AND I WILL MAKE OF YOU A VOWEL SOUND

MORAG ANDERSON

First published 24th of May 2024

Published in the UK by
Fly on the Wall Press
56 High Lea Rd
New Mills
Derbyshire
SK22 3DP

www.flyonthewallpress.co.uk
Print ISBN: 9781915789266
EBOOK ISBN: 9781915789273
Copyright Morag Anderson © 2024

i.m. Kevin Higgins (1967-2023)

CONTENTS

A WOMAN STOPS WRITING A POEM

By a narrow window blistered with rain
   a woman stops writing a poem about the past,
     trawls the contours of her brain
for the rusted key to a locked chest.
   The future kicks at the bolted door,
     restless as a stabled mare.

Barefoot, she steps into the broad swathe
   of her sea-carved island. A raw squall collars light,
     rainbows the harbour centre-stage.
Unchurched and difficult to bridle,
   she follows a froth of just-snapped stalks
     through the brandied birch of Bluebell Walk.

The wind—an unbroken colt—bucks east,
   draws forgotten women from hollow trees.

LITTLE CUCKOO

Your mother fought, I'm sure,
but lost to slack white jaws—
tongues sharp and thin as fish bones .

There is no 6am tick of water
warming pipes in this care home,
dank and foul as rotting colons.

I would feather a nest for you,
Little Cuckoo, bring a feast of worms,
but my blackbird beak is crammed with stones.

NONE OF THE NINE WERE THERE
after Maria Elena Cruz Varela

When the iced skin of December snow
latticed thighs with a trickery of cuts
thin as justice,

when festive rigging on spruce and fir
blurred trembling stars, colluded
to darken all known paths,

when a low-sung bellow, drawn like thirst
from an empty well, couldn't cross
the throat's threshold,

when the red light of retreating cars
was thrown twice as bright
against gabled granite,

when the crow unfolded wings
and swept, black as extinction,
from the telegraph wire,

when spittle from split lips foamed
and gathered like blow spray,
hit sudden as sleet,

when the raider disappeared, swift
as a conjurer's scarf,
up the alley's narrow sleeve,

when his scent—livid as pond scum—
hung like a wet pelt
on every unslept night,

all nine were busy
stitching rules into the seams
of bleeding wombs.

THE SHOPLIFTER

Flaccid light and piss-reek
seep in from the communal hall.
It takes both cold hands to form a grip,
turn the key, unlock the door.

The kids still asleep in a pleat
of thin limbs under sheets and coats,
and a lanced heart nailed to the wall.

I take the pack of sausages
from the waistband of my skirt,
bend carefully to pick apart

damp knots in oversized boots
but still dislodge the bloodied wad
of my makeshift sanitary pad.

I slide down the wall, pull my knees
to the ladder of my ribs, and bleed.

YOUR MOTHER STANDS ON THE NORTH-EAST SIDE OF THE HOUSE
after Zaffar Kunial

Your young mother ruins her only shoes
crouching for hours in rainwater
on the north-east side of the house.
Nimbostratus bruises plume under
woollen cuffs pulled over thin wrists.
Break-blackened fingers probe beneath
split lips, explore the exposed-bone surface
in her swollen basket of teeth.

Forced to fit inside the ribs of *bitch*
whose *tc* teaches her the asylum
and deceit of a well-dug ditch,
the rocky ou*tc*rop's quartz defiance.

She ha*tc*hes a plan to rise from this mulch—
taller and straighter—a resurrected birch.

A GIRL LIKE ME

She's throwing bricks, splintering the door
of the lad who calls her Pape-Slag-Bitch.

She wears anger like blood—
a constant throb beneath the surface—
seeping through second-hand clothes
slack as grey bandages.

She joins the *yellow cushion club,*
heard it will help her talk proper,
doesn't yet know she'll be maimed by laughter
from the sickle-tongued teacher.

I tell her to rise early, look directly
at the grapefruit sun, declare it
no longer bitter. Elocute,
or execute, with pencil on paper.

LITTLE WREN

Secretive songbird
wintering in dense tangles
first to sing in Spring,

rise on eagle's wing—
clever little cave dweller—
to wear the king's crown.

ON BEING ASKED TO WRITE A POEM
FOR 1983
after Jack Mapanje

From memory's brine I try to drain
a sweetmeat of the coal town
I chose to forget: the gleam
of trombone slide or trumpet bell
delicately held in thick fingers,
the tongue-slick of lips as brass
draws breath from smutted lungs.

But the hooks and teeth of 1983
cleave to pitch-black passages
dead-ended with shouts of scab!
And all I recall is a pithead
slumping into soil, uncaged men
double-bent with fear and doubt
drowning slowly in Sweetheart Stout.

MANDY AT NUMBER 9

Dry-mouthed from want of milk she learns to fear her mother's breast,
masters the art of watchfulness through a deadlocked pupil.

Hobbled by birth's random hammer, she shift-shapes unseen—
a cloud moving through rooms cold enough to snap childhood bones.

In class, Miss Vale swipes lice from her hairline, teaches her
to wash her glass eye, sneaks a clean skirt from lost-and-found.

Mr. Gaul at number 6 gifts size 5 boots. She kicks a burst ball
on concrete streets—twelve metal studs dulled to nubs.

She ferrets bottles from the bin outside William Hill's,
trades them at De Lucas' van for two scoops in a single cone.

Thursday, she closes the door to the welfare officer.
Her mum grips the handle of her mug like a knuckle duster.

PORTRAIT OF MY FATHER WITH A SAW
after Leo Boix

The new baby powder-blue.
Curtains pulled, hearth doused,
the house cold till the box is cut,
and a small grave dug.

Milk insists through cotton .
Mother scrapes the grate
with a buckled spoon,
smoors steadfast pain
with a blackened goose-wing,
a plume of ash with each dry sob.

All the lock-jaw night
Dad saws sorrow into short planks,
hands raw from sanding.
Twelve nails seal the lid,
another buried in his boot
lest he should find comfort.

Loss—a thorn that cannot be drawn
by clenched teeth
or the heat of a daughter's need.

WHAT AILS THE GIRL?

After she bends the elbow a few times,
she sees things—rats, bats, roaches.

A sock in the kisser is **the** only thing
that'll bring her out of it.

If she isn't drunk and **crying**,
she's hungover and arguing.

One minute **she** gets sore and won't talk,
next she's making a play for you.

I **got** her appetite up—scratch, kick, bite.
A wild cat, smells blood,

gets **up** on hind legs and thinks she can walk.
Can you blame me for getting rude?

Her kind's a dime a dozen.
I knew someone like her a long time ago—

little and skinny, real fireball, knockout.
A regular hellion. **Stuck**

a knife in me once. I had to smack her,
get **it out of** my system.

I gave her the first drink, now I can't stand
a dame that's drunk. Turns my stomach.

If ever the time comes when her kind can walk
a city street in daylight with nothing to **fear**—

HOLLOWING A MOUNTAIN

i.m The Tunnel Tigers

You blast one stubborn day from another,
chisel sombre chambers from granite.
Water, loosed from singing burns above,
seeps through jewel-blue crevices
where rowan roots anchor against winter.
Its steady drip cools your sweat.

Shift's end, you shoulder the pick—
the shatter of rock still ringing—
and emerge to St Fillan's unreliable dark.
Wind curves gullies, hums like a struck bell,
echoes your belly, hollow as the carved hill.
Hunger lingers on limbs like dew.

Stars partition the sky like Stations of the Cross,
the last wash of light offers itself west.
You walk worn muscles to the corrugated camp,
pray for sleep's deep trench, stroll with me
on Donegal's bladderwrack shores.
But this far from home, God is small and frivolous.

THE UNHEARD TESTIMONY OF
AGNES WILSON

When the last of the drinkers
sinks into waxen skin, adrift
like sea-wrecked timber,
and tinkers leave the tavern
to sing in darker corners,
you smoor the fire—bank heat
for travellers asleep in rented cots—
swing open the door to empty
the night's slops from a tin pail.

Grappling hands clamp your mouth,
yank fistfuls of hair from your scalp,
tear your apron, rip through linen
to the stained scraps of an underskirt.

Young voices skid like stones on ice,
break without forecast.
The first kick from a boot,
the second a shod hoof.

Forced astride a knotted trunk
lashed to the flanks of restive horses,
you are driven past the kirkyard's towering ash
to the southern edge of the village.

Left to repent by the naked trickle
of Cessnock Water, the raw rage
between your legs subdues
the ripening bruises on your back.

Lads of the Auld Licht,
she has always lamented
nights spent serving
foul ale and stale flesh
to your fathers.

THE FULL TENDERNESS OF PARTING
for Highland Mary

Bleak Greenock morning skulks the empty dock,
herringbone sky billows like the Nancy's sails.
Magpie on the windowsill holds light hostage,
comes to watch my lungs drown. Breath stumbles
barefoot through the stubble field of my breast.
Chill October shawls my collar, carves my joints
like the River Coil snaking Mannochmill.

In the trysting thorn's fragrant shade
my love deflowered a harebell, crushed
plum petals between finger and thumb,
scented my hollows with adder-grey water.
The mite who pricked my skin with bible verses,
set flesh to flame with lingering pledges,
leaves me here to moulder in silent dust.

HUNGER FOR A FRUITED THORN

for Jean Armour

As though thumbing plump fruit
for ripeness, you palm me this way
and that. Words unlace restraint.
I walk the tightrope of lust, taste
the pale froth of short-lived bliss.

Our trysting hour quickened
by morning's first blush,
I urge young heat upon you.
My cheeks' flush outbids the sun
as I steal a path home through birdsong.

Night after night you rub against rock,
shed old skin for the pink of new.
Deceit falls from your lips
like seeds from a blackbird's beak.

And, still, I want you.

A STUDY OF ANGUISH

'And poetry will raise its lamp amidst the woods'
                                        - Vítězslav Nezval

Spring, fool dark seeds to burst with abandon,
etch me in fern fronds of opaline frost,
quicken the riddle of first-light birdsong,
velvet me, naïve, in Swan's-neck Thyme-moss.
Rouse the river's copper rocks with snowmelt,
set square the bone-grey sky with Svalbard geese,
crown granite corries with morning's lilac,
souse me under clouds of blackthorn's promise.

First, free me of the blade in winter's eye
that switches my skin with willow branches,
slices a thin day from the shank of night.
Remember me as the season passes—
drunk on the ruby bloom of squandered days,
sweetly debauched by the forest's decay.

CORMORANT SPEAKS

Barefoot in mudslick streambeds I pathpick over rotsoft limbs, wade neckdeep in suncold loch, seek forgiveness. Feet leave silt—I am held. On a rockspit, Cormorant sits wingspread. Speaks, *there is still some way to go, you may have to swallow stones.*

Placid & alone,
rise from dark spine of water.
Wind dries fallen leaves.

NO ORDINARY TUESDAY, 2001

Though I am late
for an intimate sweep,
I cannot turn my back
on the woman pressing

the hem of her dress
between gripped knees.
She steps off the window ledge.
I lift my keys and leave.

A traffic warden slips a ticket
beneath my wiper blade,
tells me my time is up.
I weigh the gravity of his words,

tear the folded paper
into yellow petals,
throw them to the air.
They rise, bloom, settle.

My September-belly swollen
with unborn child.
While we are all free-falling,
she begins her first descent.

I WILL STITCH WITH BRAIDED SILK WHEN I AM GOD

Act 1
I turn day into night.
She numbers the colours
of a distant winter.
Light leaks beneath taped lids.

Act 2
I press a blunt-edged blade
through Her swollen walls.
She underscores the sapphire floor
of a chemical heaven.

Act 3
I stand firm, feet planted
on solid ground.
She swims through lavender fields
past trees heavy with sweet fruit.

Act 4
I am the greater light
in this sterile room.
Lesser bodies satellite,
await the arrival of Her star.

Act 5
I delve with unstained hands
to deliver a monster
from the pale warmth
of Her primrose waters.

Act 6
I fasten gashed flesh
with braided black silk.
She has multiplied
and replenished the earth.

Act 7
I rest and know no pain.

DAUGHTER, HOW WILL I KNOW YOU IN THE UNDERWORLD?
after Eavan Boland

Morning noise staggers through the ward—
a chainsaw-throb behind my ears.
Motionless as a crease in the hospital sheets,
I am a forest without trees.

In the next bay a milked mother strokes
a muzzle-soft fontanelle.
A helium balloon pinks the dividing curtain,
hisses a quiet deflation.

Envy clings
like gauze to a weeping wound.
The midwife's pity is real but distant—
the flaked gaze of a plaster saint.

The solitary brilliance of rage
craves colour, marches Halloween-red
through constricted vessels,
lodges in my heart's left ventricle.

Violet in my arms, I know your silence
before I know your name.
Nightly, a vulture on a thermal,
I turn the five corners of a circle.

MIGRATION
for Jesse

Long after my shelterbody shucks
        her reluctant skull
                from my shell,

her foetal cells—
        rosefoamed in my core—
                migrate to mend my flensed heart.

Drawn to salt tides
        and moondipped pools,
                she bends east with scatterlight,

forgets to look west
        where night falls last.
                Distance turns everything blue.

I peel a pearldom of song
        from my mothertongue,
                seal it in bottleglass, send it

on the carryingstream.
        She grasps freedom,
                swims her own rhythm.

I name the space between us
        Brokenwater. Claim it,
                Beautifuldaughter.

SHOULD YOU ASK
after Eugenio Montale

I am not at a table,
slick with spilled beer
and glass-eyed students,
sucking a flux of ice
from the mouth of someone
who is not yet my lover.

I do not want
these threadbare days
of marbled silence—
me, the rusted iron barb
of a neglected fence,
you, the snagged fur
of a mountain hare.

BY THE RIVER'S COLD MOUTH

How quickly snow ignites the old scene
        beneath the bite of a boiled-skull moon
                the blackthorn winter we spent, closer than kin,

coaxed from fields by the urgent bloom
        of damp skin in an upstairs room,
                the slow yoke of bones we could not name.

Your milk-and-honey confidence
        tracked autumn's swaying lantern west,
                sweetened the fabric of unmade beds.

I learned the weight of summer's loss,
        sang with a voice resigned to smallness
                and ripened our unshared harvest.

Rooted by the river's silver fork,
        I am living by the tick of a stopped clock.

NIGHT SWIM

I inch
into ink, feel
the loch's fist
clench my chest.
I do not resist
but submerge
to the cool tomb
of smothered sound,
expunge day from lungs.
Spill-of-milk moon
billows on my swell,
fills my mouth
with twilight. From
the wood's edge
he watches me
net a shoal of stars,
knows the coldest
are never
blue.

LAST BOAT HOME

for Katherine

'Bear these words in mind
as they bear me soundly
beyond my reach'
                    - W.S. Graham

Though I fade like sailors' footprints,
            do not moulder
                        under grief's woollen blanket.

When the ocean knocks at your wind-scraped door
            rise to greet me,
                        the first Atlantic bite.

When simmer dim's lamp is trimmed bright and clear,
            find me trailing west—
                        the last knuckle of light.

When words freight your untilled tongue,
            sit by a rogue of stones at Scurrival
                        and sing.

In the bittersweet lull between two days,
            open your mouth
                        to salted air—

and I will make of you a vowel sound.

NOTES

Page 8: A response to the Brown Babies Digital Exhibition curated by Professor Lucy Bland. An estimated two thousand children were born to white British mothers and black American GI fathers during the Second World War, half of whom ended up in children's homes.

Page 9: A response to the American Supreme Court's overturning of the Roe vs Wade ruling; influenced by Maria Elena Cruz Valera's *Kaleidoscope*.

Page 11: A response to Zaffar Kunial's *Foxglove Country*

Page 14: A response to the title of imprisoned Malawian poet Jack Mapanje's, *On Being Asked to Write a Poem about 1979*. 1983 saw the beginning of pit closures in coal-mining communities across Britain.

Page 15: Mandy grew up on the same housing estate as the author in the 1980s. An excerpt from the Scottish Child Abuse Inquiry, 2016, reads: *Vast numbers of these families were scattered throughout the community and their filthy habits, their maladjustments, their irresponsibility, and their neglect of children came as the greatest of shocks to those who saw these evil things for the first time.* (Allen and Morton, 1961: 51)

Page 16: A response to Argentinian poet Leo Boix's poem *Portrait of my Grandfather with Scissors*.

Page 17: A found poem from the script of John Huston's 1948 film *Key Largo*

Page 18: In memory of the Tunnel Tigers—Donegal men who endured dangerous and harsh working conditions during the construction of Scotland's pioneering hydro-electric schemes.

Pages 19, 21, 22: Three poems commissioned by the Scottish Poetry Library for Burns Day 2022. Written in the voices of three females who featured in the life and works of Scottish poet Robert Burns.

Page 23: Epigraph from Czech Poet Vìtêslav Nezval's *Strangers' faces*.

Page 28: A response to Eavan Boland's *Eurydice Speaks*

Page 30: A response to Italian poet Eugenio Montale's *Don't Ask*.

Page 33: Epigraph from *Letter VII*, W.S. Graham.

ACKNOWLEDGEMENTS

Thanks are due to the editors of the following publications in which some of these poems, or versions of them, have previously appeared: *Butcher's Dog Magazine, Gutter Magazine, Popshot Quarterly, The Broken Spine, Pure Slush, Beyond the Swelkie, Scottish Poetry Library, Dreich Press, Not the Time to be Silent, Ver Poets Anthology.*

I am grateful to the Scottish Poetry Library, who supported and encouraged my written response to the works of Nan Shepherd and Robert Burns—several of the commissioned poems are included in this chapbook.

No small gratitude is due to my mentor and friend, Audrey Molloy; to Joelle Taylor who taught me to be *active in the cinema of my own life*, and to the late, great Kevin Higgins, whose workshops birthed many of these poems.

ABOUT THE AUTHOR

Morag Anderson was the 2023 Makar of the Federation of Writers (Scotland). Author of *Sin Is Due to Open in A Room Above Kitty's* (Fly on the Wall Press, 2021), Morag's poetry has appeared in literary journals and anthologies including *Butcher's Dog, Gutter, Popshot Quarterly, The Scotsman, The Darg*, and *Beyond the Swelkie*. The Scottish Poetry Library commissioned Morag to respond to the life and works of Nan Shepherd and Robert Burns.

She was placed in the Oxford Brookes International Poetry Prize, the Edwin Morgan Trust Poetry Competition, the Scottish Poetry Library's Best Scottish Poems; and named Over the Edge Poet of the Year and twice shortlisted for the prestigious Bridport Prize. She collaborated with three other poets on *How Bright the Wings Drive Us* which won the Dreich Alliance Chapbook Competition.

She was featured poet at the Phosphorescence Poetry Reading Series, produced by the Emily Dickinson Museum, and the Yehuda Amichai International Poetry Festival in Galway.

X: @morag_caimbeul

About Fly on the Wall Press

A publisher with a conscience.
Political, Sustainable, Ethical.
Publishing politically-engaged, international fiction, poetry and
cross-genre anthologies on pressing issues. Founded in 2018 by
founding editor, Isabelle Kenyon.

Some other publications:

The Sound of the Earth Singing to Herself by Ricky Ray

We Saw It All Happen by Julian Bishop

New Gillion Street by Elliot J Harper

Imperfect Beginnings by Viv Fogel

These Mothers of Gods by Rachel Bower

The Unpicking by Donna Moore

The Sleepless by Liam Bell

The Finey by Rachel Grosvenor

The Naming of Moths by Tracy Fells

Snapshots of the Apocalypse by Katy Wimhurst

Demos Rising edited by Isabelle Kenyon

Exposition Ladies by Helen Bowie

The Process of Poetry by Rosanna McGlone

Climacteric by Jo Bratten

The State of Us by Charlie Hill

The Dark Within Them by Isabelle Kenyon

Social Media:

@fly_press (X) @flyonthewallpress (Instagram)
@flyonthewallpress (Facebook)
www.flyonthewallpress.co.uk